The Civil Rights Movement

by Benjamin Rice

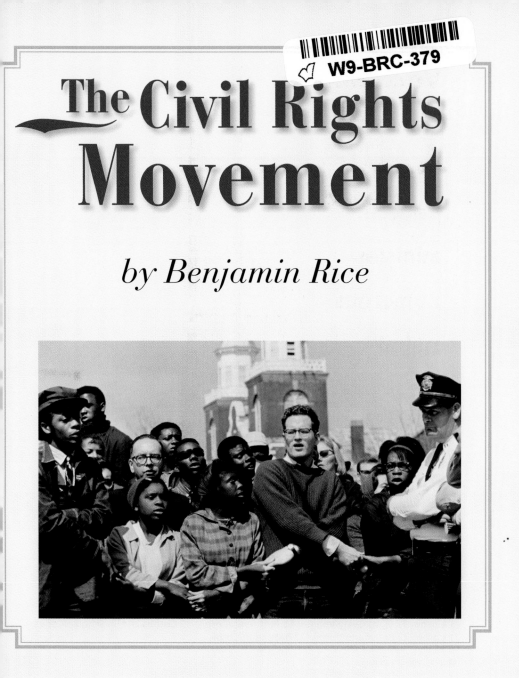

PEARSON

Scott
Foresman

Editorial Offices: Glenview, Illinois • Parsippany, New Jersey • New York, New York
Sales Offices: Needham, Massachusetts • Duluth, Georgia • Glenview, Illinois
Coppell, Texas • Ontario, California • Mesa, Arizona

ISBN: 0-328-13488-0

It was Thursday, December 1, 1955. A middle-aged African American woman named Rosa Parks boarded a bus. She had finished her work for the day as a tailor's assistant at a department store in Montgomery, Alabama. She was going home. The events that followed would become part of a long and determined fight for equality by African Americans and equal rights activists. Parks, and others like her, would stand by what they believed in to gain equal rights.

Rosa Parks takes her seat.

A Single Act

Rosa Parks was riding a bus during a time when the South was segregated. This meant that black people could not use the same public places as white people. Black people **avoided** many private businesses such as hotels and restaurants. Parks found a seat in a part of the bus where black people were allowed to sit. Then a white passenger boarded, but every seat in the bus was filled. The bus driver asked Parks to stand so that the white passenger could sit, but Parks was tired from work and would not get up. As she later explained, "After I had paid my fare and occupied a seat, I didn't think I should have to give it up."

Signs show segregation (below; top right).

Parks was arrested. When she called home, her mother quickly got in touch with E. D. Nixon, a train porter and the local leader of the National Association for the Advancement of Colored People (NAACP). Nixon worked with others to organize a one-day bus boycott to protest Parks's arrest.

The one-day protest turned into a yearlong strike. African Americans walked, carpooled, or took taxis. The buses that ran were nearly empty. Eleven months later, the U.S. Supreme Court, our nation's highest court, ruled that Alabama's segregated buses were against the law. Separate seating on buses in Montgomery ended. A victory had been won in this fight for equality called the civil rights movement. African Americans were beginning to gain rights that their **ancestors** had never had.

The Early Years of Martin Luther King, Jr.

Martin Luther King, Jr., had grown up in Atlanta, Georgia. He was the first son of a **minister** and a teacher. Young Martin spent many of his early years at Ebenezer Baptist Church, where his father, called Daddy King, was minister. Daddy King delivered sermons from his **pulpit.**

Like **numerous** black children, King learned very early about discrimination, or not being treated fairly. When King was six, a white friend told him that his mother would no longer let them play together. King's mother explained how slavery had taught many **generations** of white people to think black people were not their equals. King's parents stressed that he was just as good as anybody else, and he should never forget it.

After college King studied to become a minister. He wanted to find a way to end inequality. Dr. King spoke to the group of people who put on the Montgomery bus boycott. King urged his thousands of listeners to come together and to work for equality.

The Reverend Dr. Martin Luther King, Jr., believed in equality for all people.

The Importance of Nonviolence

From his reading and experience, King came to believe that violent acts would not help black and white people live together in peace. At Crozer Theological Seminary in Chester, Pennsylvania, King studied the life and work of Mahatma Gandhi, an Indian leader. Gandhi had used acts of nonviolence, such as boycotts, strikes, sit-downs, and other peaceful forms of protest, to help win India's independence from England in 1947. Gandhi believed that love was a force that could be used to overcome evil.

In 1957 the Southern Christian Leadership Conference was founded, partly to put Gandhi's ideas into widespread practice. Gandhi's nonviolent ideas would soon be practiced all over the South and the North. Nonviolence contributed much to the success of the civil rights movement in the United States.

Mahatma Gandhi believed in peaceful forms of protest.

Sit-Ins and Freedom Rides

In the South one could not avoid places where laws separated white people from black people. Dissatisfied people now began to test the laws that kept black and white people separate. In Greensboro, North Carolina, on February 1, 1960, four local college students continued to sit at a lunch counter after being refused service. They came home that night as heroes. By the end of 1960, more than seventy thousand people had taken part in sit-ins, like the one the four college students had put on, all over the country. Planning these different actions was the Student Nonviolent Coordinating Committee (SNCC), a group started by mostly Southern students.

Also, in 1960 the Supreme Court ruled that segregation, or keeping black and white people separated, on interstate buses and trains and in other public spaces was against the law. To test this ruling, mixed groups of volunteers rode on buses through the South as Freedom Riders. Federal officials tried to get Southern state officials to protect the riders, but local police failed to do so. One bus was even set on fire.

After the Freedom Rides and numerous demonstrations, many civil rights supporters were no longer willing to wait for gradual changes in the nation's attitudes toward segregation and injustice.

In Charlotte, North Carolina, students participate in a sit-in at a lunch counter as part of a protest.

The March on Washington, August 1963

On August 28, 1963, about 250,000 Americans, black and white, young and old, gathered at the Lincoln Memorial for a day of speeches and music. The purpose of the event was to show support for civil rights measures before Congress. Guests included a Freedom Rider representative named Diane Nash, and Rosa Parks, the soft-spoken woman whose brave act had helped lead the way.

The day ended on a high note as Martin Luther King, Jr., came to the speaker's stand. His famous "I have a dream" speech told of his dream that one day all people would be treated equally. He spoke of a day when people would be judged by who they were on the inside and not by the color of their skin on the outside. He spoke of a day when all people would live in freedom in this land we call America. His powerful words drew great enthusiasm from the crowds of people.

The march on Washington

With All Deliberate Speed

In 1954 the Supreme Court had ruled that segregation was against the law in public schools. The Court said that schools that were supposed to be "separate but equal" were in fact "inherently [in themselves] unequal."

In 1957 Central High School in Little Rock, Arkansas, became the first big test case for bringing black and white students together in school. Many white people did not like the first nine black students coming to Central High. In the end President Dwight D. Eisenhower brought in both the Arkansas National Guard and soldiers from the 101st Airborne Division to protect the nine students.

All nine Supreme Court judges agreed and ordered schools to desegregate, or stop separating black and white students, with "all deliberate speed." Little Rock decided to close its schools rather than obey the law. Progress was very slow at first. By 1964 only 2.3 percent of all schools in the South had both white and black students.

The National Guard and U.S. soldiers protect black students known as the Little Rock Nine.

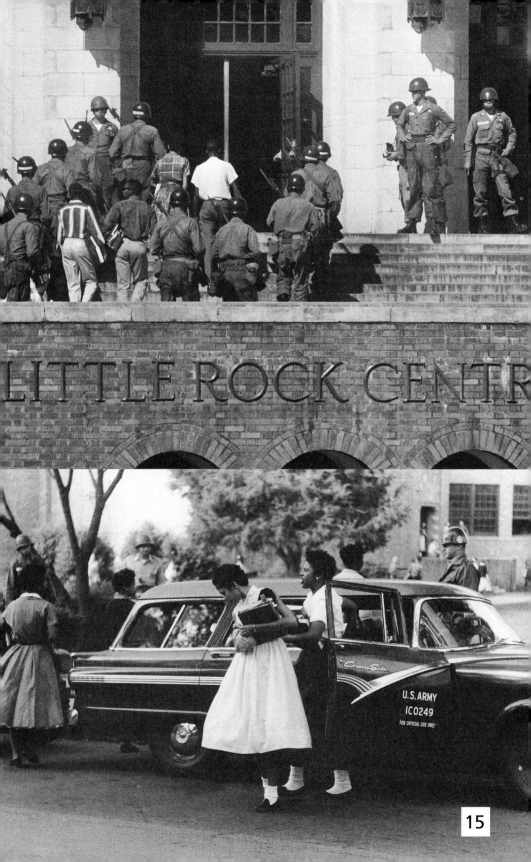

Affirmative Action

The Civil Rights Act of 1964 had high goals, just as the goals were for integrating schools, or bringing black and white students together. This act did not allow discrimination in places such as jobs or public areas. To make sure that this law actually increased equality in jobs, President Lyndon B. Johnson extended a program that had begun under President John F. Kennedy and was later expanded under President Richard Nixon. It was called affirmative action.

Under this program, employers would have to show how they were increasing the number of jobs offered to minorities, such as African Americans. Such steps might include increasing job interviews from African American colleges, or asking African Americans to take tests to become military officers. Affirmative action greatly increased job opportunities for African Americans. The overall purpose of the program was to end discrimination for anyone applying to school or looking for a job.

Men, women, and children from different backgrounds work, learn, and play together.

Voter Registration and Freedom Summer

The African American struggle for voting rights in the South has perhaps been more successful than the fight for school integration. The number of elected African American officials at all levels of government has gone up over the last thirty-four years. In 1970, there were only 1,469 African American officials in the United States. Today this number has risen to more than 9,000.

African Americans register to vote.

Prospective voters take an oath.

   In 1964 only 40 percent of the black population of voting age was qualified to vote, compared with 70 percent of the white population. There were many reasons for this. In Mississippi less than seven percent of the black people who could vote were registered. Many black men and women who wanted to vote were told they would lose their jobs if they tried to register. Others were not able to pass unfair tests. During the summer of 1964, SNCC brought almost one thousand student volunteers to Mississippi. Their job was to register voters, run "freedom schools," and start a political party.

Peaceful marches for civil rights were often met with violence. The general public became angry at the lack of response from the federal government. More than five hundred protesters, with nothing **shielding** them but their belief in equal rights, set out from Selma, Alabama, on March 7, 1965, to Montgomery. State troopers attacked the peaceful marchers with clubs and sent them back to Selma.

Eight days later, President Lyndon B. Johnson spoke to a special session of Congress. He promised to give a law to Congress that would end the difficulty African Americans faced in voting. He explained that African Americans want "to secure for themselves the full blessings of American life. Their cause is our cause, too."

Civil rights marchers unite in Selma, Alabama.

President Lyndon B. Johnson

The Voting Rights Act of 1965 would greatly change the power of the African American voter. The act banned the tests and other measures whose purpose was to keep African Americans from voting. If states continued to turn away African Americans who wanted to vote, the federal government could send in people to register them. By the year 2000, 66 percent of all eligible African Americans were registered to vote, and 53 percent voted.

The Continuing Struggle for the African American Equality Movement

Martin Luther King, Jr., was a civil rights leader whose ideas appealed to white and black people alike. In 1966 he joined the Chicago movement, which was fighting for fair housing policies in that city. Before he was killed, King was preparing to lead a strike by garbage workers in Memphis, Tennessee.

Even before King's death, however, the mood of some civil rights workers had become angrier and less open to nonviolence. Riots in various cities across the United States made the need for nonviolent change more obvious, yet more difficult. The mood of the country was also divided by the Vietnam War.

Florida Supreme Court Justice Peggy A. Quince, 2000 (far right)

Former Secretary of State Colin Powell (left) and then
National Security Advisor Condolezza Rice (right), 2004

Today the achievements of the civil rights
movement for African Americans are clear: a
better-educated, higher-paid African American
population; a much higher percentage of
registered African American voters; and sharply
higher numbers of elected African American
officials. Civil rights organizations continue to
fight for the rights of African Americans and for
other minorities as well.

Some people have perhaps forgotten the way
things really were in the days before civil rights.
White people who committed crimes against
black people were not punished back then. It
was a time when black people every day, in small
but important ways, were made to feel less than
equal. Because of the civil rights movement,
those days are now largely over.

Glossary

ancestors *n.* people from whom you are descended.

avoided *v.* kept away from.

generations *n.* people born about the same time.

minister *n.* member of the clergy; spiritual guide; pastor.

numerous *adj.* very many.

pulpit *n.* the platform or raised structure in a church from which the minister preaches.

shielding *v.* protecting; defending.